Autumn Blaze

Leena Thampi

© **Leena Thampi 2021**
All rights reserved
All rights reserved by author. No part of this publication may be reproduced, stored in a retrieval system or transmitted in any form or by any means, electronic, mechanical, photocopying, recording or otherwise, without the prior permission of the author.
Although every precaution has been taken to verify the accuracy of the information contained herein, the author and publisher assume no responsibility for any errors or omissions. No liability is assumed for damages that may result from the use of information contained within.

First Published in May 2021
ISBN: 978-93-5427-485-5

BLUEROSE PUBLISHERS
www.bluerosepublishers.com
info@bluerosepublishers.com
+91 8882 898 898

Cover Design:
Mohammad Fayez Zameer

Typographic Design:
Ilma Mirza

Distributed by: BlueRose, Amazon, Flipkart

But I, being poor, have only my dreams; I have spread my dreams under your feet; Tread softly because you tread on my dreams.

William Butler Yeats

Content

Prologue 1

Royal suite 3

A luxury that only a few can indulge in. 3

Bury the Hatchet 7

Words treasured for the intellectuals 13

Till Eternity 17

Legacy 20

I can't be a Living corpse. 23

The Musk is in the umbilicus 26

Motherhood 29

We will Rain together 31

My Haven 33

The Scent of Desire 35

A hand that fed milk 37

Fragrance of January 40

Celebrate the fall 43

Perhaps her soul kept running ahead of her
body without quitting 45

Bonded forever 47

To crave and to have are just like to see a thing
and it's Shadow. 49

Weeds at stake 51

The Alchemy 55

Beyond the scream 59

Gift me the prophecy 62

Light a lamp for the world. 66
In Trance 69
Two Different views 71
Silence: The most beautiful voice 77
Don't steal my view, be a part of it. 79
Blended them 81
Don't let the child inside you die, for it teaches
you how to live. 85
My Refuge 88
My Heart is a Museum 91
A museum without walls. 91
She used words to say nothing andSilence
to Explain everything. 93
She waits for a glimpse of him, with the
kohl in her eyes. 96
Once Bitten, twice shy 100
My Life Tags 105
Filling the Blank pages 107
Vintage Lass 109
A Sand Castle built on the shore of my heart. 112
My Soul needs an escape. 116
Autumn Blaze 120
Don't want to step out of this ambience. 123
Discomfiture 125
Palette of colors 127
The greatest oak was once a little nut who held it's ground. 129
Outgrow the seasons 131
Your journey is different because you are unique. 134
-Dreams Never Die. 137

Goddess is the epitome of femininity *139*

*If there is another life, I would still be your
little princess: My Dad* *143*

Strange Indeed *145*

Yes, I am a Phoenix Bird *147*

*Hey men! grow up, don't abandon good women
for a temporary slot* *150*

Listen to your intuitions *151*

Such a Drag *153*

Autumn Blues *155*

Autumn Bliss *157*

Prologue

It is not empty
Every falling leaf
is a poem
A mystery
Carrying pleasure or pain
Every falling leaf is a blessing
It falls, in a divine place
To rise again beautifully as an Autmn Blaze!

May be my soul was too deep to explore

So, I painted the wall in my room with the letters hidden in my heart,

I stitched my dress with words from the books I read.

Wore it with elegance and pride.

This is where I live and what I wear.

Frosted glasses, steaming coffee and

A book by my side,

Either you can step in or stroll by

But don't judge me for who I am

Royal suite

A luxury that only a few can indulge in.

Autumn blaze

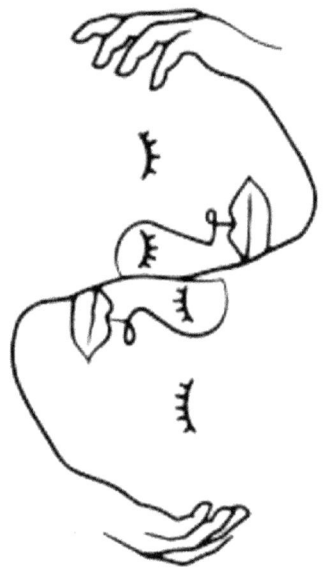

Her heart was weeping like an infant,

Seeking a mother outside in the dark

To come and sing a lullaby to soothe her sorrows and put her demons at rest.

Where did she accept her defeat?

Was it a battlefield of rattling shields?

Weapons failed and strategies won

Emotions had no values against the swirling swords,

She read somewhere, that the enemies throw phrases and wavering facts,

And every book she read tumbled on her

from her arranged shelves.

Conceding her defeat, she surrendered

And kneeled to the ground.

Found her truth lying in the mud

Shattered like a house of cards.

She tried to fix her fragile body back.

With all the pain oozing out in vain,

She cherished her wounds again,

No proofs, no witnesses to proclaim

Cause she knew her conscience

Had won the battle at last.

Bury the Hatchet

Autumn blaze

The Holy Basil in my courtyard never dried,

I always watered and lit a lamp,

Which remained glowing till late night,

Resonating so many hopes in my heart,

Sat back watching the beautiful

Queen of the night and the shy

Jasmine buds waiting to bloom,

The combo danced in the air with

Intoxicating sweet fragrance,

That magic aroma from the incense burnt,

Created an ambiance that is still alive

The hymns I chanted, purified my heart and soul,

As I circumambulated the deity thrice.

My heart seeking salvation intact,

Never touched it with a muddy mind,

Lest I lose the touch of the divine,

Now imprisoned here within the four walls, I look back at the glory I lost

Take me back there once more, oh lord!

My heart craves to rekindle those memories galore.

Ancestral Home

Autumn blaze

The words unattended and unwritten,

Cried out, breaking the silence

Then slept on it for a while,

Withdrawing to the conch

Its flared lip whispered in resonance,

Why would I be written in a book

Where it is gone unnoticed and ununderstood?

Words treasured for the intellectuals

I might leave you and go one day,

But you will hear me in the words of our special song,

That we used to sing all night long

You will find me in the unfinished paintings,

And the words scribbled in my Diary,

And in the crumpled-up papers where I wrote it all wrong,

I lay there in between the pages of your book

As a peacock feather there you look,

In the fragrance of jasmine left on the pillows,

Pieces of my bangles you broke with your hugs,

Memories we shared wrapped in six yards laid,

With the gifts I showered whispering my name.

Jingling anklets will dance in your mind

And you'd hold your fire long to feel my wet tangled mane,

Giving you that winking smile.

I will taunt you with the naughty question again..."Do you love me"?

Just to remind you, that my soul can't be tamed...and I will be the same.

Till Eternity

Autumn blaze

He was an ordinary story

She turned him into a classic one

Worth reading.

May be each life is an echo of the ones

That came before bouncing off

The things they learned to land on a new dais.

The truth is unveiled then and that's how he understood his worth.

As books remain even after we fade,

That's why we write our names on them to be remembered.

So, we leave a taste of who we were on our cover page.
She leaves a trail of her in all the things she loves,
That's how she wants to live,
That's how she wants to be remembered.

Legacy

Autumn blaze

I used to dislike being sensitive
And though it made me weak
But take away that single trait,
And you take away the entire ME.

You take away the very essence of who I am,
You take away my conscience
You take away my ability to empathize
You take away my intuition
You take away my creativity
You take away my humanity
You take away my deep appreciation for the little things in nature,
You take away my transparent inner-self
You take away my keen awareness of other's pain
Yes...you take away my passion to live.

I can't be a Living corpse.

Serenity is the goddess of wisdom and virginity.

Those who are blinded, don't have the innermost eyes to see.

Sometimes she witnesses the water bleed,

And wonders how dare they dip their crimes in holy water?

She speaks in cries more than words

Then go around searching for a needle in the hay stalk.

Whilst class of a kind, a breed apart, never let her hair down,

Cause the road of Vermillion leads her to the divine path.

They might have tasted her dignity from far.

Her heart was built to hold compassion more than a human being can measure

No secret sin of bonding dwelled in her.

Ask the Gods they will answer

Every doubt you carry about her.

Gods might have walked through the way she had

Though temples neither lie nor admit the fact.

Where sanctity is the last word not proclaimed.

The Musk is in the umbilicus

A Bird has been waiting to see her eggs hatch,

She sat day and night, spreading her wings over them to give warmth.

One fine day innocence sprouted and cried out,

*She poured her sweat throughout to nurture them strong,
And kept watching when the wings would come out.*

*The day finally arrived and left her with a heavy heart,
She could do nothing but sit and watch them fly high,*

Cause it was her who taught them how to spread the wings after all,

A voice within her whispered,

"I can bear the pain of separation sweethearts but never your fall".

Motherhood

Autumn blaze

I dipped my brush into your soul

And painted a rainbow in the sky,

Now it seems we are living an illusionary life.

As artists in the open air who wants to go too high.

Traveling through the clouds

Dig into the bark of my strength, with all the vibrant colors,

We shine and mesmerize.

There is still nothing as magical as you and me, in the entire universe

We will Rain together

Autumn blaze

I can hear your voice whenever the wind blows,

I know snow doesn't make noise, or am I hearing my heartbeat?

I am hiding here in the serene flakes

Feeling the fresh smell of fluffy cakes, tickling my nose.

I feel so peaceful and in bliss,

Would love to bury my worries beneath

As it melts, will disappear along with it.

My Haven

Autumn blaze

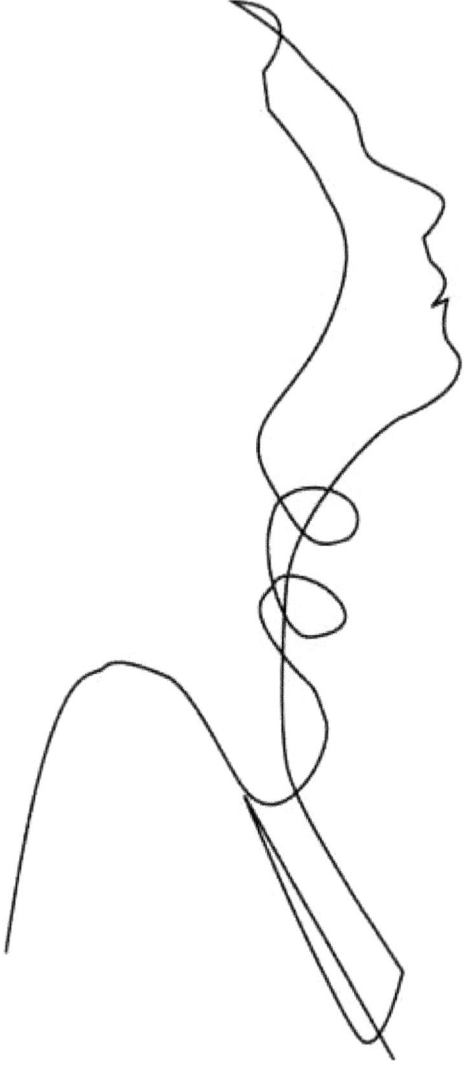

Her Dreams had fragrance

She burnt them to build up her beloved.

Carrying the soul within her bones she asked herself,

Did the sacrifices were worth it?

The question is dangling in front of her eyes, like a pendulum,

Yet a puzzle she chooses to leave unsolved.

No, women are not born to be failures,

Some treasures are buried underground,

Not to be Excavated or found

With all Luster and glory

The Scent of Desire

She stumbled upon a wounded snake one day,

She dared not touch

She was frightened,

She tried to move past holding her breath

She suddenly realized it isn't fair to leave a creature bleeding there,

She brought it home and showered her care

Till she could see the snake swirling well.

She befriended it taking for a god until she got her final love bite.

A hand that fed milk

Autumn blaze

Lost in your thoughts

Slept on the dream's shoulder

How long I kept awake

Looking ahead to you

Living and dwindling with the same hope.

Oh January, bring blessings galore

Fill my bags which I want to share,

Don't leave me empty-handed

At your door.

As I leave December behind.

Take away all worries masked beneath,

No victims should prevail and bleed

Let those wounds heal with savor indeed.

No haunting ghosts to invade

Stuck up in the cobweb here

Don't leave me like a question dear.

I am a beautiful thought that's far away.

Keep me close, my divine year.

Fragrance of January

Autumn blaze

Go leaf-peeping on your way home from the apple orchard
Take a detour.

Carry my words in your heart and see the beautiful fall foliage along.

Jump into a pile of leaves

Make a necklace out of maple leaves,

Listen to the rain on your roof, the most soothing sound in the world.

A cup of ginger tea, gramophone on

How cozy with those blankets wrapped on

Crispy Autumn makes me insane,

I wish it was fall, all year round.

Why does it make me nostalgic honey?

It is not the falling of leaves that pains me

But our own falls.

Celebrate the fall

The aches and pains in her body
Didn't know she could dance
And the dormant words didn't know
Her heart could wake them up into poetry.
No eyes could see what talents were hidden behind,
No ears could listen to the creaky sounds the bones made,
But that's how we are prepared for the long race.
Yet she oozed out and floated
With a zest to leave a print on the sand.
Can you see the color?

Perhaps her soul kept running ahead of her body without quitting

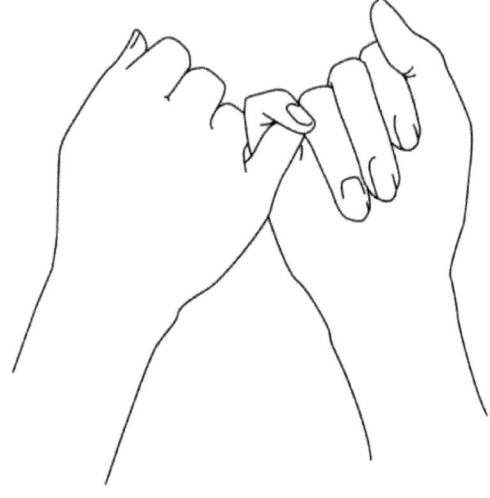

Whenever I stand up for what is right,
I end up knowing who my real friends are,
I might have walked down the lane alone,
Just to return hand in hand
With integrity and virtues as pals.
But no grudges left at the end
And all I could see that I've come so far.

Bonded forever

Autumn blaze

He asked her to give him an eternal space in her poetries and paint him on the walls of her memories.

And that's what she did exactly!

To crave and to have are just like to see a thing and it's Shadow.

Autumn blaze

He planted a seed of reincarnation in her mind
Not knowing that it went dead out of suffocation
Without water even before it sprouted.
She wished he knew only divine things grew in her garden.

Weeds at stake

Autumn blaze

I found in her a reflection, a solace
Like a soothing breeze,
Like a dandelion wish,
Like a morning dew,
Like a spring in the desert,
Like the sky lives in the sea,
Like a sweet unheard melody,
Like a peaceful meditation,
Like an angel in dreams,
Like a melting idol of snow,
Like a soul awakened
Like a prayer fulfilled,
Like an unaltered prophecy!

Inexplicable connect

I don't think I have met you
But I have read you somewhere.
I have heard you somewhere
Like a great taste in music
I find you somewhere in those lyrics
That character in the Book
The literature you choose
Those flavors that tease my taste buds
The fragrance that tickles my nostrils,
Yet unknown but known
Where are you?

The Alchemy

I sit across the mirror, face to face

To have an open conversation

A good listener, I thought

But if I am not there to talk

Who would talk to you?

Who will smile at you?

And make you happy?

I promise I won't let

You ever feel empty.

Are you scared of me?

Or from my authenticity?

Hope I don't look ugly...

And you convinced me, divinity never,

You know, the day I changed

Was the day I quit trying to fit into the world

That's never really was mine.

You stood there holding every fear

Every beautifully broken piece of mine.

I have decided to be silent

Cause the words seem too powerless.

But I am sure you can hear my scream.

Beyond the scream

Autumn blaze

I felt the sea was always panting in my conch,

A ceaseless whisper which I held very close to my ear.

Yes, only I could hear those chants,

My bones were disintegrating,

As I sat there on the tip of an iceberg, heartbeats floated about on clouds strumming harps.

Before I slip back into the sea of the unreal.
I regained my soul,
Don't betray me and I cried aloud,
For you are that one thing I am proud of,
And I seek no reincarnation.
When I cannot predict the real anymore.

Gift me the prophecy

Autumn blaze

I have a light that God wants me to let shine,
it's glowing inside
Without flickering, burning bright,
Showing me the way through
dark, dusty gloomy roads apart.
Don't worry, even if your own
shadow leaves you,
Go light a lamp for yourself.

Light a lamp for peace and love

When the world starts closing in on you,

Light a lamp that shines all the way around the world,

This is the only way, to reach every heart that cries somewhere alone.

My lamp has a flame which never extinguishes,

Cause it's him who is fueling it day and night, all the year-round.

Light a lamp for the world

Autumn blaze

A portion of me was taken away
Which I had treasured in a chamber of my heart.
Those pages were not for sale,
But for the one who could enter and read it well
And read without stealing it from there,
It was inscribed in golden ink.
A dialect which I wouldn't share,
Is there anyone who could decipher them,
And dwell there forever?
I still have pieces of love in my body.
If ever you are reborn, I want to meet thee again.

In Trance

Autumn blaze

He was in love with her silhouette,
She was in love with the sunrise and sunset.

Two Different views

Autumn blaze

I sit in silence, In a dim-lit mood,

While into the darkness I cast my stare.

I understand the language of nature

The language of wind.

It's like silent music to my ears,

The speech of the sky is manifested through the raindrops,

Though the clouds silently try to

hide them behind

The rainbow shows its subtle expression through the colors,

Sun takes a dip silently into the sea.

Yes, I can visualize the dumb silence of slumber or apathy,

As femininity become silent, shyness becomes her language

That artist's canvas speaks to me in his aesthetic language.

Is that what you call a baffling silence?

I can sense the noisy silence of resentment in her anklet.

She seems lost and forgotten, her good old days remind her of her passion.

I have known the silence of the stars and the sea,

There stretches the longing silence of the desert,

Tormenting to quench its thirst.

Or is it the fertile silence of awareness

Pasturing the souls?

Only I can hear that echo at the mountain side, they too have tears which flow with the lakes

.

Listen to the silence of the city when it pauses, for a while I too need a nap it laments,

Yes, the silence of the sick in the hospital room sucks,

I have felt the silence of suppressed aches and pains,

The stitches on the body could not cry aloud but only smiled.

Have you ever felt the silence of

Words unuttered and the loss unmoaned?

Out of such chaos, when we survive

We realize that we are neither devil nor divine.

How dare we raise a voice when silence seals every single sound!

No words could ever meet the wealth of the world of silence.

For it is to be pure and holy.

As I sit here in my solitude bliss,

I hear distant lyrics to a song, a song that

Sounded as if it was coming from

Silence of the calm open sea.

I love this silent symphony

It is as deep as Eternity.

Conversing in a void, I find myself

Though it bleeds a million times,

Until my heart has expressed itself,

A silent prayer is sent upwards

Even God doesn't understand the words spoken out loud,
He understands the wordless thoughts
We carry in our eyes, because
Silence is a divine language.

Silence: The most beautiful voice

Autumn blaze

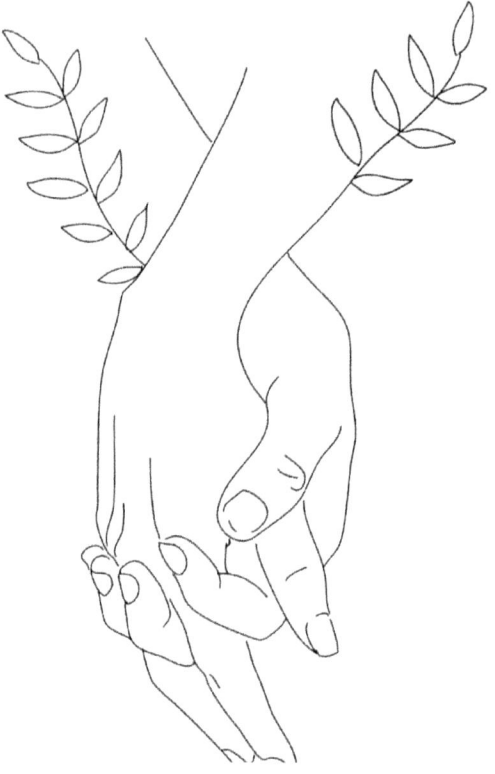

I was in my world,
Enjoying this rare beautiful view,
Where rain encountered the sun,
That's when the cloud intruded in
To put a damper on,
Grabbed my sun to create a rainbow
In their land.

Don't steal my view, be a part of it.

Autumn blaze

Words were offended with bells yesterday

"She abandoned me and held you close" maybe it's the gesture play.

But that's not how it goes, I whispered

My dance is a poem, where every movement is a word.

The sound of the bells replicates my heartbeat,

The musical rhythm coincides with my breath,

Every move, I make, take me to a world, I have fallen in love with

My world is filled with art where everything has a sacred place.

Blended them

Autumn blaze

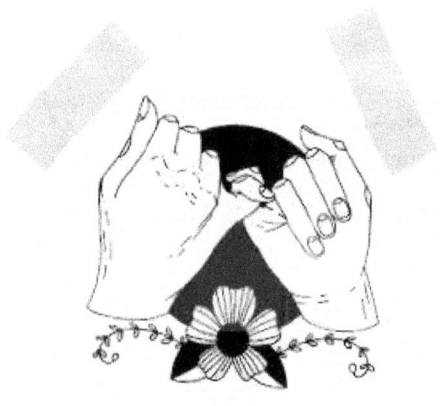

I know a small girl who lived in me,

She squealed in delight when she's happy

She cried whenever she was hurt,

She never had insecurities and inhibitions,

Neither gave a damn about society.

She was unbiased and honest sans boundaries

She believed in angels and fairy tales

She always looked up to a shooting star

And wished all that her innocent heart yearned.

Then, one day she had a nightmare

That her fairyland is getting demolished

She ran away and hid.

I am searching the child everywhere

Can anyone help me with her address?

I cannot live without her here

I am sure she's alive somewhere near.

I cannot let her die since I am matured,

I know, she can't match society's standards but she's my sole life and inexplicable happiness.

Don't let the child inside you die, for it teaches you how to live.

Be Bonded like the serene waves that touch the shore

For they never cease to care or bid adieu.

To me, the ocean is more than a dream,

They come and embrace the land in the vicinity without any secret intentions.

The sun witnesses the beauty before the world merges in the dark.

The echo of the tidal melody resonates with the depth of trust and harmony.

Here I stand untouched by ego, greed, and pride.

I am nothing but a void,

Who is ready to gulf into those big flows?

Unburdening my mind, as I return home

I visualize the sun in my mind,

Feel the wind in my hair, taste the salt on my lips and my soul bleeds into poetry.

And every time I return, I find my tranquility in the twilight.

My Refuge

Autumn blaze

In this world where everyone seeks novelty,.
I am in love with the antiques.
Where do I stand?

My Heart is a Museum
A museum without walls.

Autumn blaze

Who says silence is silent?
Listen to silence silently
Sit and lend them your ears
Listen to what the words fail to say
At times they make the words jealous.
Silence puts the words to shame.
Words that are seeking ways to come out loud
But my mind still stays to be quiet.
And silence silently wins the game,
Smile sweetly and Strides away.

She used words to say nothing and Silence to Explain everything.

Autumn blaze

Once again, she concealed her poems
Beautifully behind her kohl
Which only her lord could read,
Hurricane of thoughts, ocean of tears
He knows her pain, he knows her cure.
He knows her dreams won't be in vain
Since she believes in the fragrance of Sandalwood paste,
Which adorns her forehead with grace
She will always be blessed with those kohled
Dove's eye: The divine gift from him,

To view the Sanctum Sanctorum at dawn

For yesterday's offerings of her lord.

When he is woken up from the deep slumber of the previous night.

He is bedecked in decorations.

The sight is so auspicious and divine.

She would never miss in her life

Yes, he Lived in her divine eyes undistracted and deep.

She waits for a glimpse of him, with the kohl in her eyes.

Autumn blaze

Recalling the encounter of wind and rain

Brings a shiver down my spine

How many spring flowers have been blown away and how many fell?

Those flowers I took care of all my life

Listened to my music they bloomed and danced,

With clear melting dew, the last petal

Bid goodbye last night.

Taking away the dust of this floating world we live in,

I stood there watching a thousand wishes scattering in the wind

Leaving traces of memories lingering in our hearts.

Is this how we meet and part?

The breeze shouldn't have been so rude, immature, and harsh.

What exactly was my fault?

Last spring everything was intact.

I dare not to plant a tree again in my yard

Since the fear of withering haunts, me throughout.

Once Bitten, twice shy.

Autumn blaze

...but love is like a rainbow.

Sometimes it appears when it's still raining, and it's just too dark to see.

And there it's gone when you want it all the more.

Accomplishments have no colour.

Autumn blaze

My Time cannot be bought
It's Intrinsic.
My Love can't be conquered
It's divine.
My Mind cannot be Bought
It's priceless.
My Body cannot be broken
It's molded.
My Dreams can't be washed away
It's anchored.
My Integrity can't be withdrawn
It's deposited.
My Happiness can't be ruined
It's inbuilt.
My courage cannot be broken
It's the spine.
My soul cannot be claimed
It's saved.

Autumn blaze

I am stuck somewhere between the past and the future,

What if, what might, what could have, and what never will.

Haunted by Words of intuition,

Flipping through the pages of the past.

Blinking at the future,

It was then the overwhelming realization hit me,

There is so much more to life

Then simply surviving it.

Let me plant the seeds today

For all the flowers of tomorrows are in the seeds of today.

Give them time to bloom,

Make an inspiring story worth sharing tomorrow.

Filling the Blank pages

Autumn blaze

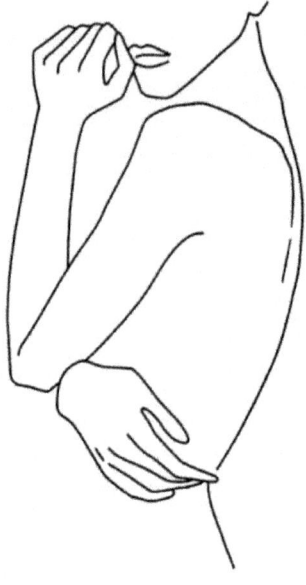

A score of years Leave vintage stories,
Faded cards,
Places are now gone.
leaving reminiscences and
The lingering vintage heart alone
Vintage sunshine
Vintage jewels
Vintage dress
Vintage fragrance
Vintage painting
Vintage music
Vintage books
Vintage love
Vintage moment
Vintage Emotions
Vintage home
Vintage artifact
Vintage memories

Vintage Lass

Autumn blaze

Like the waves that touch the veins of the shore,

Your caresses keep me intact,

Leaving me with this quivering frosted shoulder every time you reach me and hug.

I might lay here bare if breeze refuses to bring you near to veil,

My arms will still reach out to you

Since my roots are strong beneath the shore

I am not prepared to seek another land
Where I should continue to be an alien.
I wish I could write your name on the strand,
But I fear the waves would wipe it off
Immortal memories should remain on the shore,
Like a beautiful castle unshaken and strong.

A Sand Castle built on the shore of my heart.

Autumn blaze

l Thought Today...why?

Why live in a world where a mask is worn over another?

Why live in a world where power and prestige overrule your integrity?

Why live in a world where selfish motives weigh more than your altruism?

Why live in a world where your sanctity is considered insane?

Why live in a world where your modesty is interpreted as arrogance?

Why live in a world where unconditional love has to pay a big price?

Why live in a world where truths are silenced by lies?

Why live in a world where guiltier dances around the imprisoned innocents?

Why live in a world where charity is made to holy places rather than slums?

God never demanded luxury, did he?

Why live in a world where Gratitude is not the crux of life?

My Soul needs an escape.

Autumn blaze

Those dreamy leaves fall from heaven

Fluttering, swirling in the breeze

Touch my face and provoke a smile

Speak bliss to me, the season of mists.

As summer bids goodbye

To the flagrant crimson.

Lurks in the dusk dancing

With the wild red leaves,

Touch my dainty feet, making a carpet so fluffy on the ground. With a thousand memories,

Every leaf touches my soul

They ask me where I have been.

The unending wait-triggered questions setting ablaze my entire being.

Answers are all buried here.

Cause it's you who taught me tolerance traits.

Keeping away demons and evils at stake.

Now I am frozen snow lying here in your embrace, my soul lulled into rest.

With the promises of a lifetime warmth.

Fall for me, my Autumn Blaze!

Autumn Blaze

It's you who make me realize that heaven is just close to me and not far away.

Don't want to step out of this ambiance.

Don't want to step out of this ambience.

Autumn blaze

Aren't you standing there like a rock, smiling or crying which I know not,

Leaving me in the dark,

You stand there in the spotlight, which I keep lighting at dawn and dusk

That one wish I ask ever since I was born,

Didn't you turn deaf and dumb

To my prayers, oh! Beloved,

When I adorned you with my garlands of tears.?

Lord grand me these alms, I am consistently at your door

No materialistic possessions I seek, but to be the epitome of Faith to the world.

Don't leave this devotee empty handed, lone and lost.

Show the world miracles do happen when we manifest them a lot.

Discomfiture

Autumn blaze

This world is a canvas
We meet and we part,
All that remains are
Traces of Brush and ink.

Palette of colors

Autumn blaze

Do not pull my roots, let me stay grounded by faith,

My children might need them tomorrow, to turn over a new leaf.

They need this soil to withstand the storms and droughts of life.

For we all start somewhere, and spread out branches wide,

Still we come back stronger together,

Cause our routes are rooted back here.

The greatest oak was once a little nut who held it's ground.

Autumn blaze

Born in the lap of nature,

Every season has its beauty, watching the trees flower,

The colors of leaves change, so do human beings.

By the time we crave more the season is overshadowed by another,

Igniting our eternal mind, all with pleasing ecstasies.

How can it be that all this beauty is a sign of death and decay?

I wish it lasted Just like the iconic waltz, not a whimsical, teenage romantic

type but A legendary classic reunion kind of immortal moves that swirl till eternity.

Outgrow the seasons

Autumn blaze

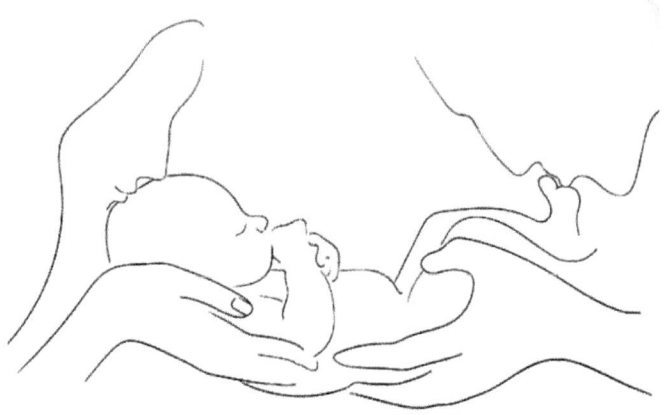

You have been at war with the world, whenever injustice finds its way to you.

You try to fight back and stand tall but you fail every time.

Again, you curse the pretense and facade, withdraw yourself to the conch.

When everyone joins hands to defeat you, let them be United

Keep your weapons down, but never surrender your values and goals.

Perhaps you have allowed too many to trespass your heart with their heavy dirty feet.

Enough is enough, now leave the ground,

You don't belong there,

You are born to win a different battle.

Where victory is embracing yourself in fighting an inner war

Why attend the battle outside?

Be the queen of your kingdom.

Your journey is different because you are unique.

Let things go wrong as they sometimes will,

Never grumble or complain keep working on...

No quitting in mind.

Even when your debts are high and funds are low,

Never lose hope...

No quitting in mind.

When you feel like ending your life,

look up and sigh

Learn to calm down the hurricanes of your mind

and enjoy your inner peace.

When you finally realise you have got nothing to lose,

you turn into a beast...

No quitting in mind.

You are allowed to scream,

You are allowed to cry,

You are allowed to rest for a while, but remember...

No quitting in mind.

Sometimes we think dreams are dead,

but you have got to wake them up

from deep slumber cause,

It doesn't have an expiration date,

so take a deep breath and try again...

No quitting in mind

All the clouds will turn and fold

Keep your mind fixed on the road

It's just the breath before the plunge

It's just the dark before the dawn...

No quitting in mind

-*Dreams Never Die.*

A woman is an encapsulation of strength, tolerance, calmness, divinity, and many more qualities that lie deep inside them.

Though not a born Draupadi, Sita, Kali, Mohini, and Savitri

But wherever and whenever they have to emerge as one, they arise and prove themselves to be an epitome of womanhood.

As Draupadi, born from the fire taught not to play with a woman's weakness by the devastation of Kauravas.

As Sita, the daughter of Earth.

Her personification of grace taught us how to be forgiving, serene, respectful, and loyal to her man.

As Goddess Parvati turned out to be fierce Kali

to fight with the demon which taught us how a woman can be both compassionate and strong.

As Mohini, the most beautiful taught us not to underestimate a woman's intellect.

She was a blend of beauty and brain.

As Savitri, the best wife ever taught us how unconditional love can make impossible things possible.

Goddess is the epitome of femininity

Autumn blaze

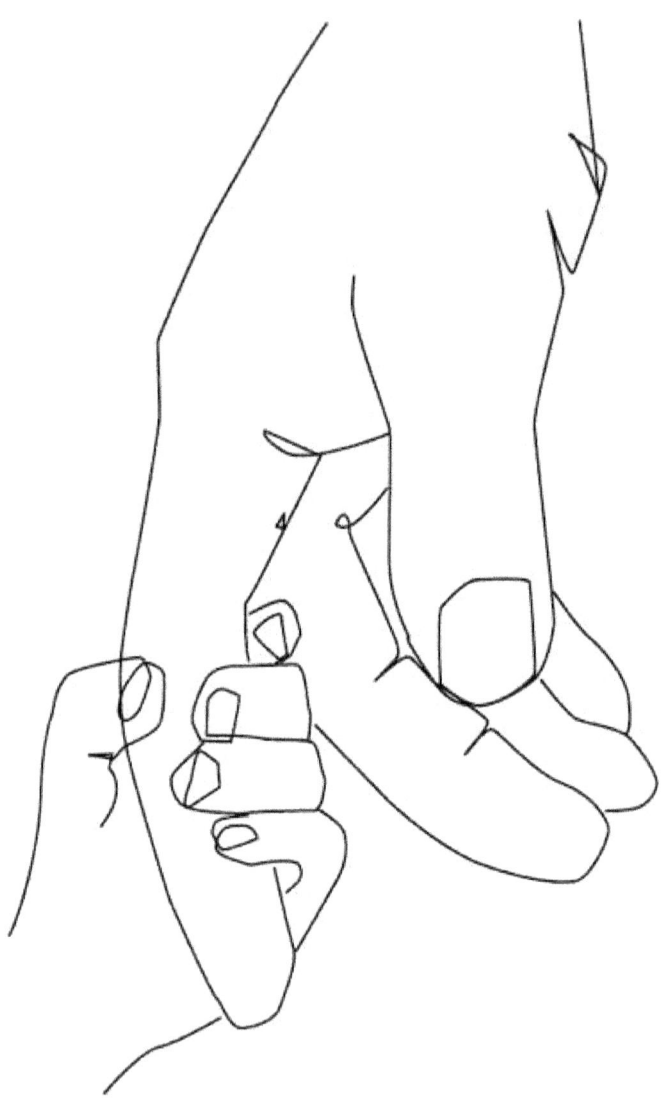

My Dad is a person who is loving and kind,

He knows so well, what's on my mind,

Whenever I stand perplexed in life,

he appears to be a blessing in disguise.

Plodding along in the daily strife

Bearing the whips and the scorns of life

Never saw him with a bad temperament though

he has always been my best friend keeping his smile alive

No slings and arrows in my life,

When I have this god man by my side.

A loyal husband, a gentleman

Any family would envy.

He never knew how to hate

And helped everyone to up their game,

I dedicate these verses and poem in his name,

Cause he's the motivation behind the same.

Only my dad, the best of men

Is a benchmark with which I measure every other man.

And I feel honored and proud to say that.

If there is another life, I would still be your little princess: My Dad

Autumn blaze

And no-one spoke and no-one smiled
There were too many spaces in the line.
I can barely define the shape of this moment in time.
The clock is ticking fast and beyond our control.

Look at the strangers we've become
No doubt, without the love we need, we're done.
Yesterday somebody asked me whether I knew you,
A million memories flashed through my eyes but I just smiled and said, I used to.

Strange Indeed

Autumn blaze

The way I love you with every piece of me,

I am sure you cannot see but feel,

Every time I give and give until I'm left with nothing

Then again, I dig back thoughts of our moments

Out of nothing, I make something to give.

I may fall a thousand times more,

To lift you and build you strong.

May I turn myself into ashes

To keep you warm again?

Yes, I am a Phoenix Bird

Autumn blaze

Someone has to tell the truth about betrayal,

Sexting," philandering, one-night standing or searching for so-called "soulmates" while being married.

What is going on in relationships today?

Lack of intellect or acting as malignant narcissistic sociopaths who are unfit for human relationships?

The answer is very simple,

They never genuinely loved the woman they married.

Just an infatuation and momentary thought which gave birth to children,

Leaving the woman an emotional prisoner lifelong.

Their children didn't know who was right and who was wrong

Hey men! grow up, don't abandon good women for a temporary slot

Don't allow others to make you or break you.

You design yourself,

You are the artist of your life.

You only know where your colors are hidden.

Paint it in your unique way.

So can you get through a sea of exclamation points and question marks?!

Listen to your intuitions

Autumn blaze

Either I am there or I am not,

Nowhere in the middle, you know.

It is those who fake a smile holding a knife behind,

Expect a corpse to dance to their tunes, and call it the way of life.

Such a Drag

Autumn blaze

Hold on tight to the tree

My clingy yellow leaf

The seasons might change

But i can't remain here without thee

Those Green leaves promise me happiness galore,

No,i don't want to climb up

and let you down

Cause today's sweet vows turn sour tomorrow.

Autumn Blues

Autumn blaze

Mid-summer, sunlight, midwinter white snow...
Fragments of love fall down during this season.
My home is somewhere here,
Don't search me anymore.
I am a living poetry.

Autumn Bliss

https://www.linkedin.com/in/leena-thampi-820476210

https://www.facebook.com/Rhythms-of-a-Heart-110653987209158/

@thampileena

www.ingramcontent.com/pod-product-compliance
Ingram Content Group UK Ltd.
Pitfield, Milton Keynes, MK11 3LW, UK
UKHW022210230426
12048UKWH00016BA/755